Hot Springs National Park

Attractions & Sights to See

Billy Grinslott & Kinsey Marie Books

ISBN - 9781965098271

Mountain Scenic Drive and West Mountain Scenic Drive. Hot Springs Mountain Drive begins at the end of Fountain Street off Central Avenue. It has switchbacks that will take you to a picnic area, the Pagoda overlook, and the Hot Springs Mountain Tower. West Mountain Drive has entrances on Prospect Avenue and Whittington Avenue. It is a two-way road that leads to the Summit Loop where you will find three overlooks that you can pull off on and enjoy the spectacular views.

Mountain Tower. The tower elevator will take you 216 feet to the top observation decks. The tower's upper observation deck is open to the air, where you'll enjoy breathtaking panoramic views of the Ouachita Mountains. You can either drive or hike to the tower. There is also a museum on the 2nd floor.

West Mountain Trails is a series of five different trails you can hike. Each trail is different in length and difficulty level. They include Canyon Trail, Mountain Top Trail, Whittington Trail, West Mountain Trail, and Oak Trail. These trails are 1.5 miles or less in length. Some are flat and easy to hike. Others are difficult and harder to hike. You can pick a trail that fits your style.

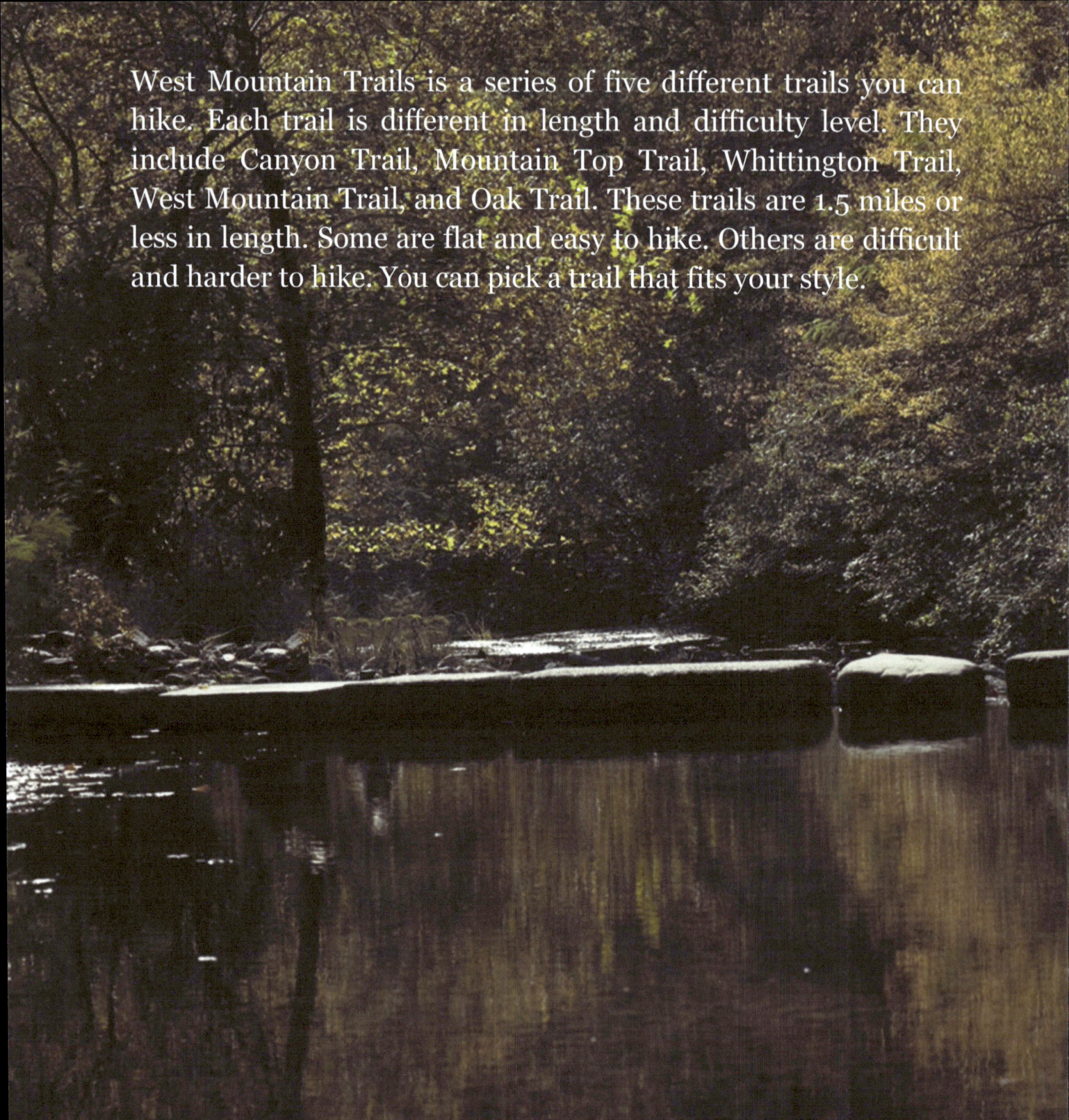

Sunset Trail is the longest trail in Hot Springs. It Crosses all types of terrain. The trail makes its way through some of the most remote areas of the park. This trail is divided into three sections. West Mountain (2.8 miles), Sugarloaf Mountain (2.6 miles), and Stonebridge Road (3.8 miles). You can choose to hike part of the trails or hike them all.

Tufa Terrace Trail. This paved trail can be reached from the Grand Promenade trail or Arlington Lawn. The lower portion of the Tufa Terrace Trail is near the Hot Water Cascade. The trail one way is less than 1/3 of a mile. The Tufa Terrace Trail passes historic Ral Spring and follows a level path across the hillside before rejoining the Grand Promenade.

North Mountain trails are a group of different hiking trails. It consists of 16 different trails you can hike. These trails are all 1.5 miles or less. Some of them connect with each other so you can visit other areas of the park. Others can be reached from other areas in the park. They all offer scenic views of the park.

Honeysuckle Trail connects Peak Trail with Hot Springs Mountain Trail. This hike primary trail can be used both directions and has a easy overall physical rating. Distance one way is 0.5 miles. This trail is best used as a route to access the picnic shelter at the intersection of the Floral Trail and the Hot Springs Mountain Trail

Fountain Trail. This short trail begins on Fountain Street below the entrance to Hot Springs Mountain Drive. Use it to reach Honeysuckle Trail. It's only about a quarter mile long and connect to the hot springs loop trail.

Floral Trail. Floral Trail connects Lower Dogwood Trail and Honeysuckle Trail. From either trailhead you will descend into a valley and climb the other side. This trail makes a "U" shape, ascending to Hot Springs Mountain and North Mountain on both sides of Hot Springs Mountain Drive.

Lower Dogwood Trail climbs North Mountain. Near the top, boulders mark the westernmost tip of the trail. From there, the trail drops downhill. Discover this 1.7-mile loop trail. Generally considered an easy route. This trail is a bit more technical than most. the added steepness takes some effort.

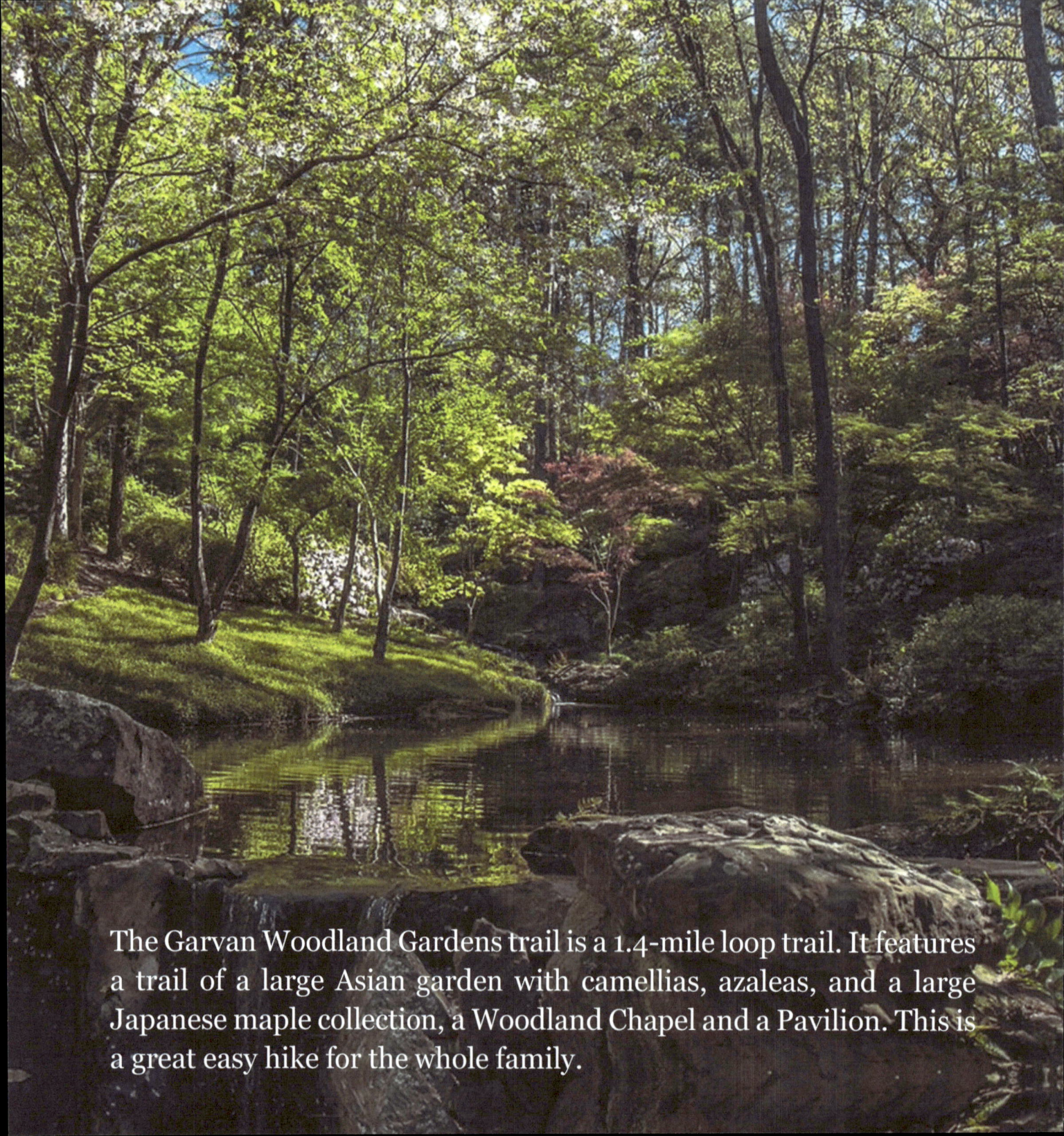

The Garvan Woodland Gardens trail is a 1.4-mile loop trail. It features a trail of a large Asian garden with camellias, azaleas, and a large Japanese maple collection, a Woodland Chapel and a Pavilion. This is a great easy hike for the whole family.

Lake Catherine State Park. The park includes a boat launch ramp, a pavilion, picnic sites, playgrounds, and a well-marked trail that leads to a waterfall. The park has 20 fully equipped cabins. This peaceful park is located on Lake Catherine, one of five lakes in the beautiful Ouachita Mountain region.

Lake Ouachita State Park. Arkansas's largest lake, it offers 40000 acres of clear, clean water surrounded by the scenic Ouachita National Forest. It offers, swimming, boating, fishing, a boat ramp, a playground and several hiking trails. The park has 93 campsites, some right on the water. Lake Ouachita is located on the Ouachita River near the resort spa of Hot Springs. Great for all around family fun.

Pirate's Cove Adventure Golf. Awarded one of the best miniature golf courses. Putt your way through mountain caves, across a pirate ship, over footbridges and under cascading waterfalls. Pirate's Cove is the ideal family activity for your Hot Springs visit. Pirate's Cove is perfect for the whole family.

The Grand Promenade is a recreation trail that runs parallel to bathhouse row. It's about a half mile long and made entirely out of brick. The half-mile Grand Promenade offers views of historic downtown Hot Springs, the Arlington Lawn, the hot springs cascade, quartz veins in the sandstone and tufa cliffs.

Magic Springs Theme and Water Park offers over 80 attractions and rides including roller coasters and thrill rides such as plummet summit and the gauntlet. Splash Island features 10 water slides, a bucket that dumps 1,000 gallons of water and dozens of ways to get wet and stay cool. It also features bubbler jets, water wheels, tipping buckets, water curtains, net climbs, pools and waterfalls. The water park also features the exciting surf simulator Boogie Blast, Kodiak canyon adventure river, seven falls body and tube slide tower, a 350,000-gallon wave pool and much more.

Fun Trackers Family Fun Park offers a go-kart track or have fun getting wet in a bumper boat. It has a mini-golf course with a fire-breathing volcano. It also offers laser tag and an all-new arcade & game room. With over 4 acres of activities, guests of all ages are sure to have fun at Fun trackers Family Fun Park.

Arkansas Alligator Farm & Petting Zoo offers guests the opportunity to pet and feed many different types of animals. It also has an alligator farm where you can feed and even hold a small alligator. It offers a family-friendly atmosphere where everyone gets to be a kid.

Ouachita National Forest is the South's oldest and one of the largest national forests. It has recreation areas such as Albert Pike, and Shady Lake. It offers campsites, fishing areas, picnic sites and hiking trails. Also available are swimming areas, hunting, fishing, mountain bike trails, all-terrain vehicle trails, and horse-riding trails. It is located about 20 minutes from Hot Springs.

Charlton Recreation Area and Camping is located about 20 minutes from hot springs. It offers around 50 different styles of campsites. It offers areas where you can picnic, swim, hike, and fish along Walnut Creek.

A Narrow Escape is an interactive puzzle and escape room adventure that you and your family can enjoy. A Narrow Escape is in downtown Hot Springs. The best escape rooms and games, great team building for family and friends.

T-Rex Laser Tag and T-Rex Fun Spot. Family Entertainment, Laser Tag, Go-Karts, Bumper Cars, Mini Golf, Rope Course and a Zip Line Course. Great fun for the whole family.

West Mountain Picnic Overlook. One of the best places to picnic in Hot Springs, this overlook hangs higher up on West Mountain overlooking the city of Hot Springs. In addition to picnic tables is a historic mountain shelter located on the left side of the overlook. You can access it by driving the West Mountain loop road.

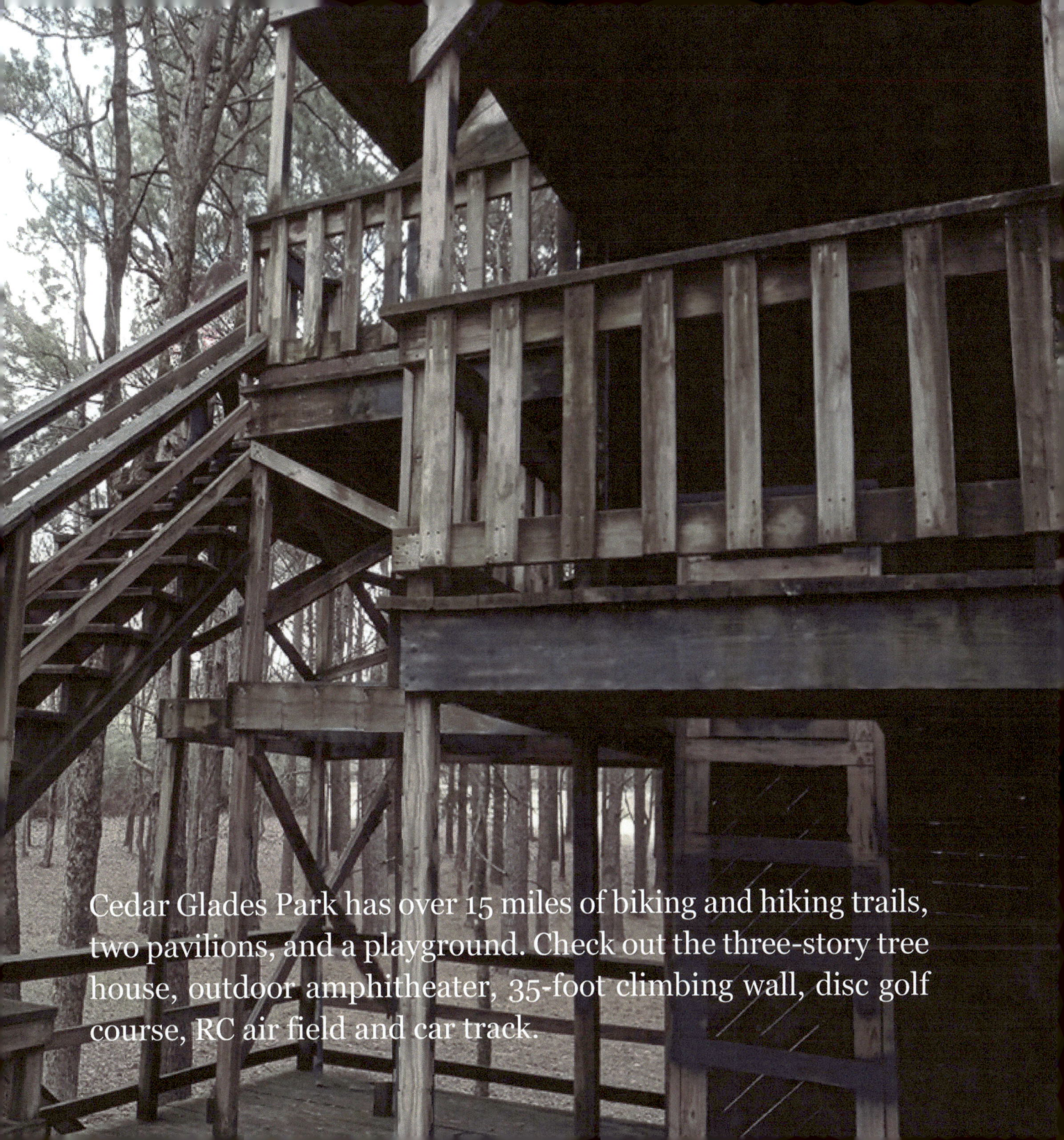

Cedar Glades Park has over 15 miles of biking and hiking trails, two pavilions, and a playground. Check out the three-story tree house, outdoor amphitheater, 35-foot climbing wall, disc golf course, RC air field and car track.

Lake Sylvia is located in the northeast corner of the Ouachita National Forest. The serene wooded 18-acre lake is great for swimming and fishing opportunities. The park has 14 campsites with water and electricity. 8 primitive sites and two group tent camping sites.

Northwoods Trails has 31 miles of mountain bike trails. The Northwoods trails includes Green, Blue and Black single track, multi-track, flow trails, jump lines and an expert section. The Cedar Glades trailhead includes a bike skills park. Bikers, hikers and trail runners will enjoy this area.

Mid-America Science Museum has over 100 hands-on exhibits, both traveling and permanent exhibits. Some include, Lost World of Dragons, Tesla Coil Theater, Digital Space Shows, and the Science Skywalk.

The Galaxy Connection Museum is a Star Wars and Superhero themed museum attraction, collectible toy store, and birthday party space. Journey back in time and see some of the most famous superheroes.

Adventureworks is an exciting zip line adventure park. An incredible treetop zipline experience through the forests of Hot Springs. You can even zipline at night when there's a full moon. Kids 12 years of age and older can enjoy zip lining.

Hot Springs Bark Park. Take your dog to the bark park and let them have some fun. The park features 2-acres of fun spaces for dogs, water stations, benches, asphalt walking paths, and more. it's operated by the city and is open from dawn to dusk.

Pinnacle Mountain State Park. This day-use park offers a variety of outdoor adventures on three converging rivers. Pinnacle Mountain State Park offers opportunities for climbing the mountain, canoeing and kayaking, hiking, mountain bike riding, and more. Besides the more than 40 miles of hiking trails, there are also the Arboretum, a playground and plenty of picnic tables. Pinnacle Mountain State Park is just outside of Little Rock Arkansas.

The Goat Rock trail offers stunning views of the Ouachita Mountains and the thermal springs. Limited parking is available at the overlook. The trailhead starts south of the parking area. It is a 1.3-mile trail with excellent views. Generally considered a moderately challenging route.

The Peak Trail leads to the Hot Springs Mountain Tower and the top of Hot Springs Mountain. Visitors can choose to stop at Mountain Tower, and take in views from the overlooks, or go the top of Hot Springs Mountain. The Peak Trail connects to a lot of the other hiking trails for those looking to explore more of the park. Nice, fairly easy trail through mostly woods.

Gulpha Gorge Trail connects the Gulpha Gorge Campground to many of the park's trails. Discover this 1.4-mile out-and-back trail, considered a moderately challenging route. Highlights include beautiful scenery, and refreshing creek views. Be prepared for a challenging and steep hike along gravel terrain that offers stunning views of the surrounding scenery.

Oertel Trail branches off Gulpha Gorge Trail and follows along the southern edge of Hot Springs Mountain. It is a 3.3-mile out-and-back trail, considered a moderately challenging route. Oertel Trail ranges from moderate to very steep grade. Challenges are steep inclines and rocky areas.

Upper Dogwood trail has short rises and long stretches of flat terrain. You can connect to the Lower Dogwood Trail or the Goat Rock Trail to create a longer hike. Enjoy this 1.5-mile loop trail, generally considered an easy route. Well-marked, well maintained. Great trail with great views.

The Display Springs are some of the few open-air springs in the park. They are an excellent place to learn about the Hot Springs thermal water areas. Located directly behind the Maurice Bathhouse, this spring runs out of a hillside and flows into a shallow pool below. Shaded by trees, this is a great place to relax and listen to the sounds of running water.

Hot Springs Arkansas

Other Things to Do

There are many other activities you can do in Hot Springs besides visiting the national park. The area offers a lot of activities, in and around the city of Hot Springs. If you are planning a trip to Hot Springs, it's well worth your time to explore what the area has to offer.

Activities in the area include, theme and water parks, biking, hiking, zip lining, miniature golf, horseback riding, fishing, camping, water sports. boat cruises, boat or jet ski rentals, helicopter rides, and more.

The area offers plenty of hotels, resorts, restaurants, arcades, laser tag, bowling, theaters, museums, area parks, picnic areas, spas & bath houses, trolleys, carriage rides, and many more activities.

NATIONAL PARK SERVICE

Hot Springs National Park

National Park Service
U.S. Department of the Interior

Author Page

Billy Grinslott & Kinsey Marie Books

Copyright, All Rights Reserved

ISBN - 9781965098271

www.ingramcontent.com/pod-product-compliance
Lightning Source LLC
Chambersburg PA
CBHW060850270326
41934CB00002B/76